DREAMGIRLS

MUSIC FROM THE MOTION PICTURE SOUNDTRACK

ISBN-13: 978-1-4234-2577-9
ISBN-10: 1-4234-2577-4

HAL•LEONARD®
CORPORATION

7777 W. BLUEMOUND RD. P.O. BOX 13819 MILWAUKEE, WI 53213

Visit Hal Leonard Online at
www.halleonard.com

MOVE
(You're Stepping on My Heart)

Music by HENRY KRIEGER
Lyric by TOM EYEN

Moderately bright

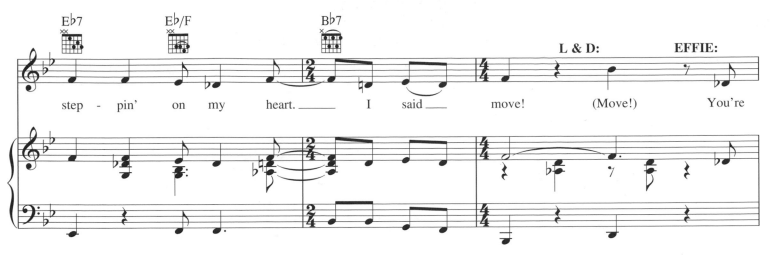

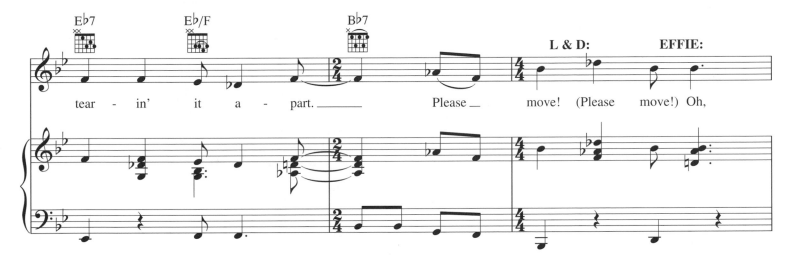

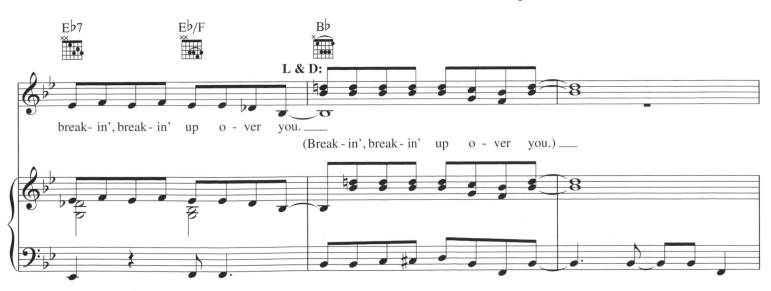

Move! Move! __ Move right out of my life! __

EFFIE:

__ You are so hor - ri - bly sa - tan - ic, the

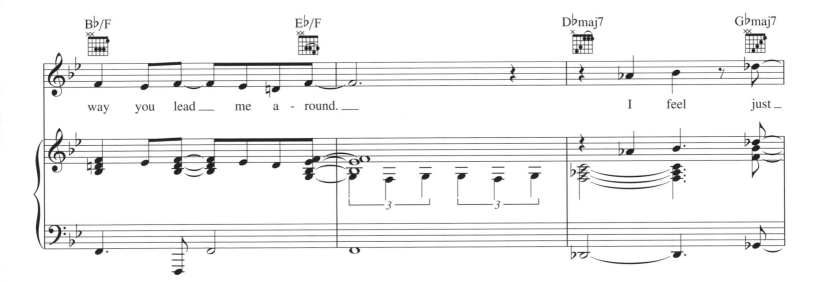

way you lead __ me a - round. __ I feel just __

__ like the Ti - tan - ic: I'm al - ways go - in' down, __ down, down. __

smell - y ci - gar, ____ and just move right out of my,

ALL:

move right out of my life. _____

**LORRELL
& DEENA:**

Please move, move,

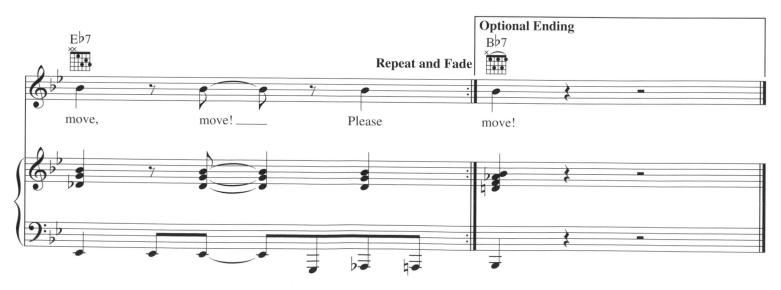

move, move! ____ Please move! move!

Repeat and Fade

Optional Ending

FAKE YOUR WAY TO THE TOP

Music by HENRY KRIEGER
Lyric by TOM EYEN

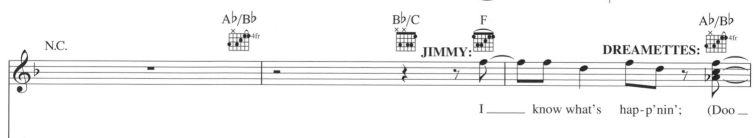

Lead vocal ad lib.

Repeat ad lib.   **Last time**

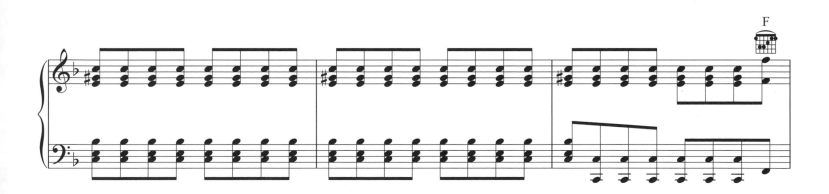

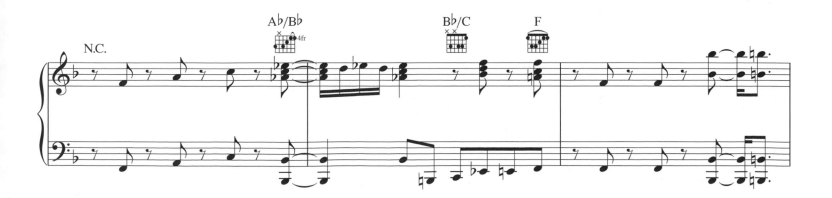

CADILLAC CAR

Music by HENRY KRIEGER
Lyric by TOM EYEN

STEPPIN' TO THE BAD SIDE

Music by HENRY KRIEGER
Lyric by TOM EYEN

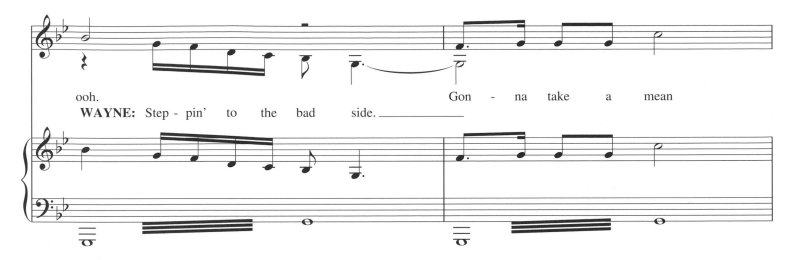

ooh.
WAYNE: Step - pin' to the bad side. _____ Gon - na take a mean

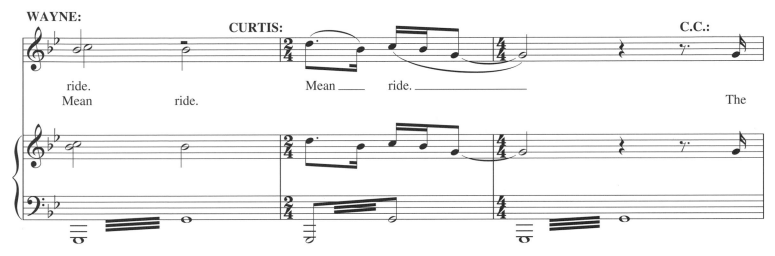

WAYNE: ride.
CURTIS: Mean _____ ride. _____
C.C.: The
Mean _____ ride.

smile I had is gone _ a - way. _____
WAYNE: Those _____ that steal are gon - na pay.

ALL: Step - pin' to the bad _ side _____ to -

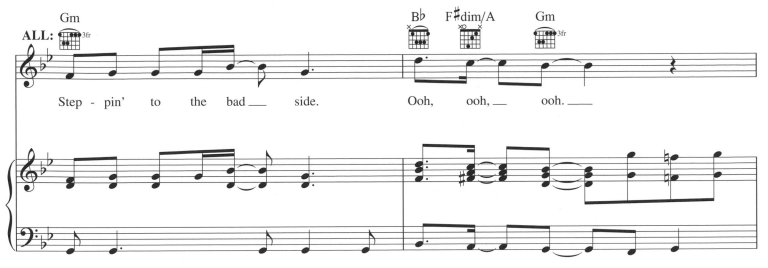

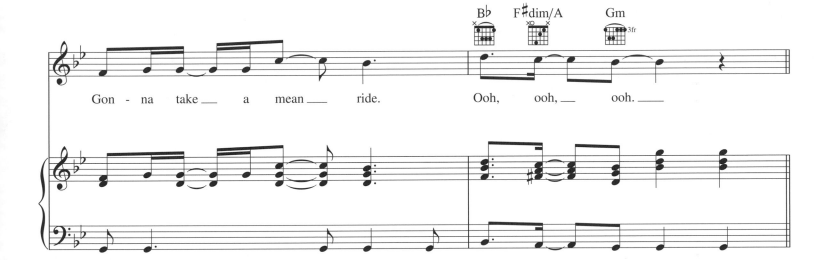

LOVE YOU I DO

Music by HENRY KRIEGER
Lyrics by SIEDAH GARRETT

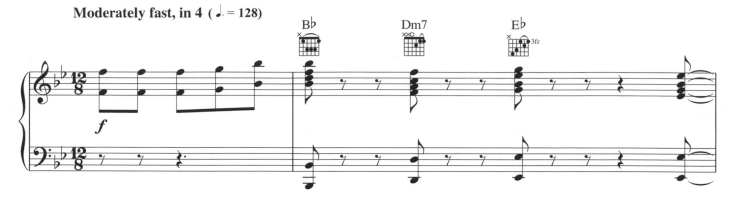

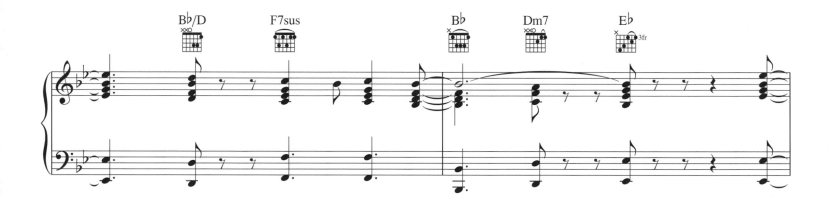

I nev-er met a man ____

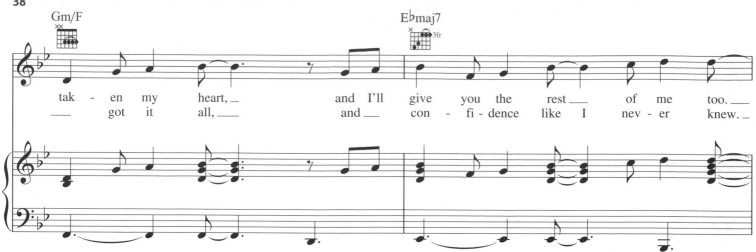

tak - en my heart, ___ and I'll give you the rest ___ of me too. ___
___ got it all, ___ and ___ con - fi - dence like I nev - er knew. ___

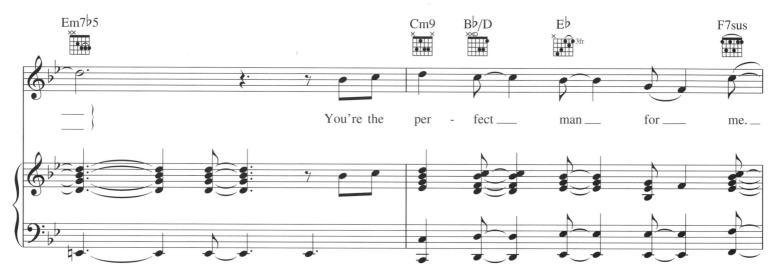

___ } You're the per - fect ___ man ___ for ___ me. ___

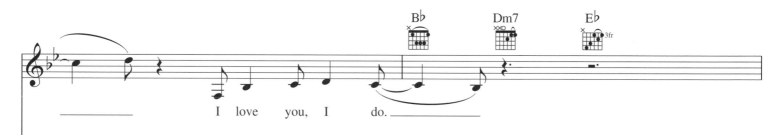

___ I love you, I do. ___

Mm, ___ I ___ love ___ you.

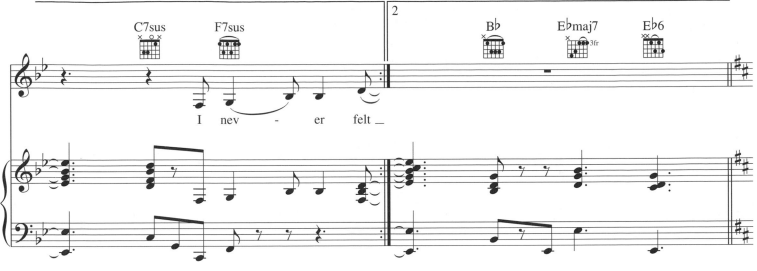

I nev - er felt __

You've got the charm, _____ you sim - ply dis - arm __ me

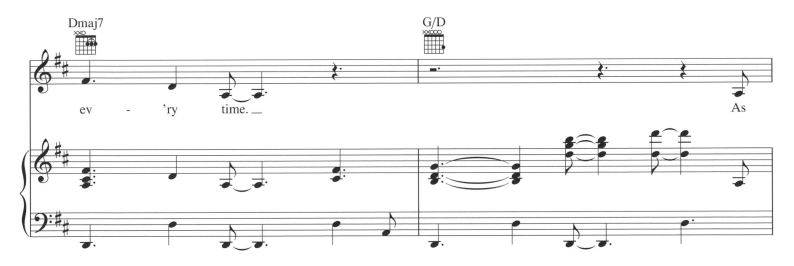

ev - 'ry time. __ As

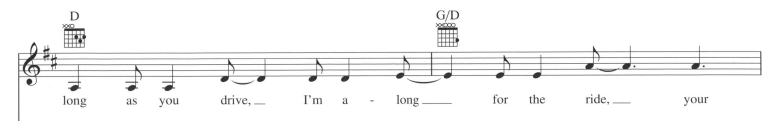

long as you drive, __ I'm a - long ____ for the ride, __ your

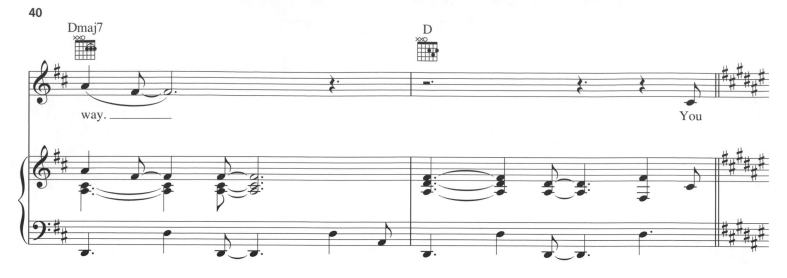

way. ____ You

said it be - fore: ___ "There won't be a door ___ that's

closed _____ to us."

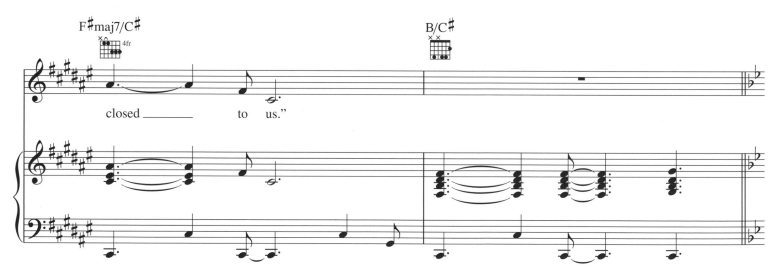

Put - tin' all my trust in _____ you, 'cause

you, you'll al - ways be true.___ Oh, _____

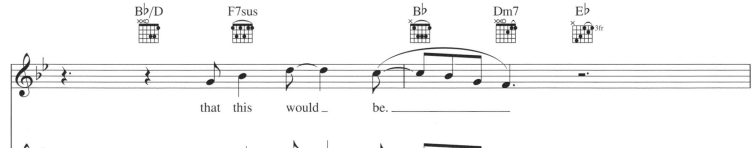

_____ I nev - er could_ have known _____

that this would_ be. _____

Oh, you, and you a - lone, _____

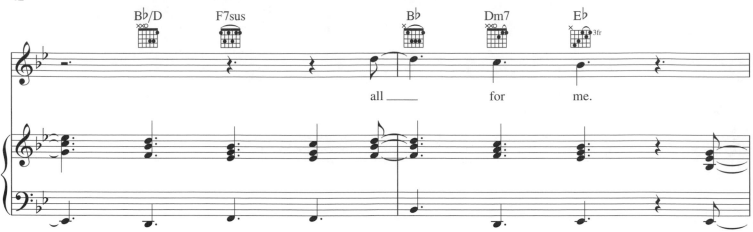

all _____ for me.

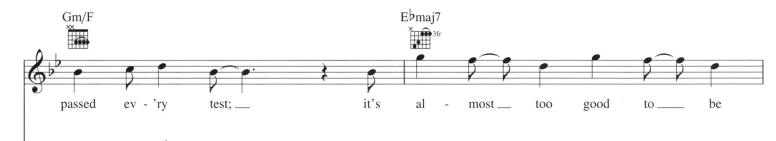

I know you're the best; ___ you

passed ev-'ry test; ___ it's al - most ___ too good to ___ be

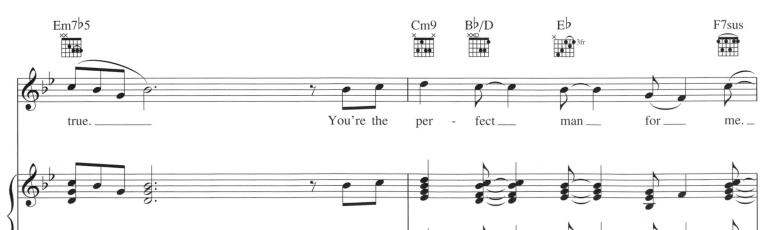

true. _____ You're the per - fect ___ man ___ for ___ me. ___

I WANT YOU, BABY

Music by HENRY KRIEGER
Lyric by TOM EYEN

ba - by, ba - by, ba - by, ba - by, please.

I know you don't __ trust the way I'm feel - ing. That's why you're stand-ing o-ver there. __

__ But, don't hold __ back __ from me, ba - by. Be -

lieve me, be - lieve me 'cause I real - ly care. __ 'Cause I

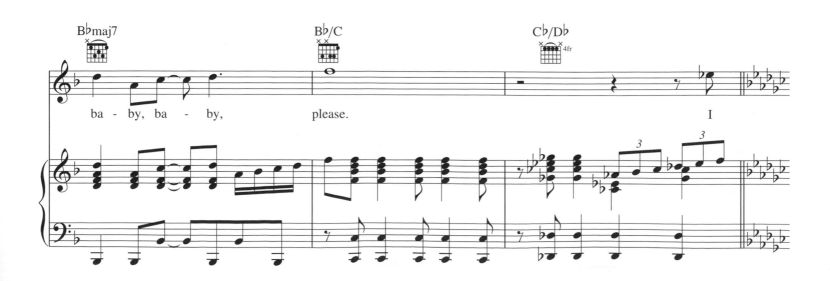

FAMILY

Music by HENRY KRIEGER
Lyric by TOM EYEN

Slowly, in 2

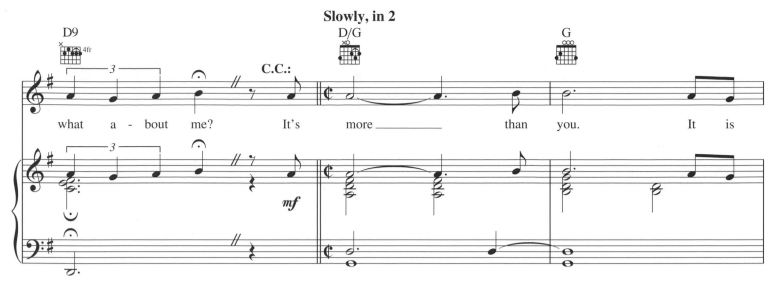

what a-bout me? It's more _____ than you. It is

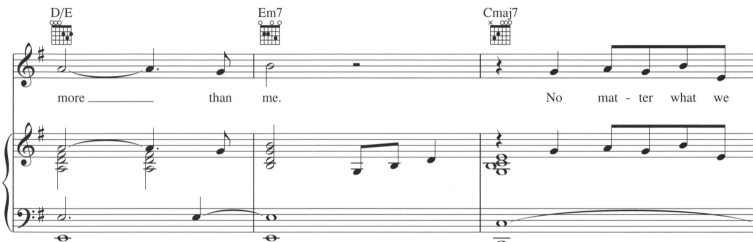

more _____ than me. No mat-ter what we

are, we are a fam-i-ly. _____ This

dream is for all of us. This one _____ can be real. _____

And you can't stop us now _____ be -

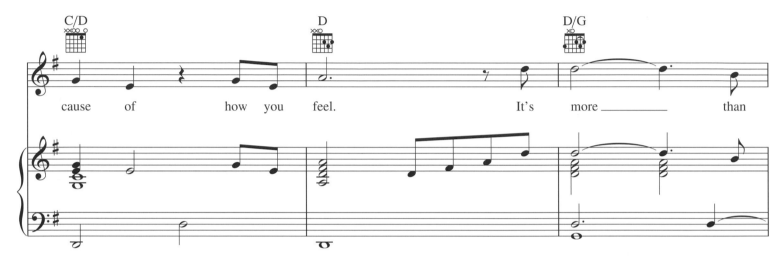

cause of how you feel. It's more _____ than

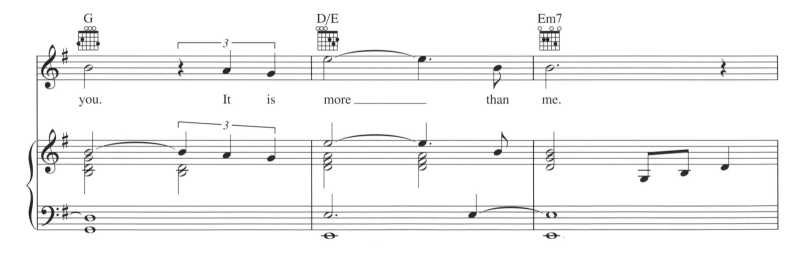

you. It is more _____ than me.

What - ev - er dreams we have, _ they're for the fam - i - ly. _____

We're not a - lone __ an - y - more. Now there are oth - ers

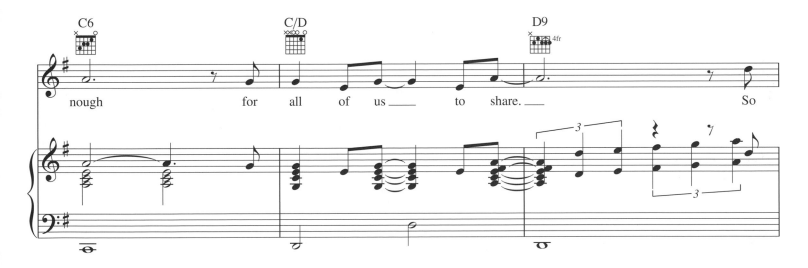

there. _____ And that dream's big e -

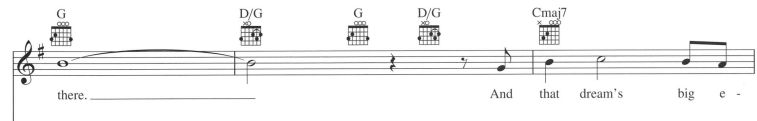

nough for all of us __ to share. __ So

don't think you're go - in'. You're __ not go - in' an - y - where. You're

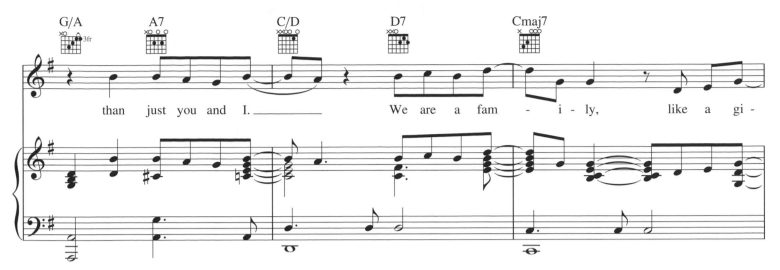

than just you and I. _____ We are a fam - i - ly, like a gi -

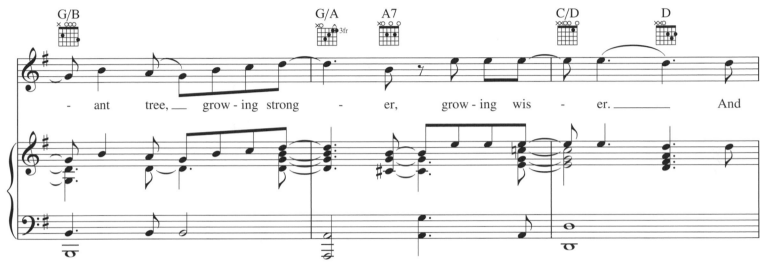

- ant tree, ___ grow - ing strong - er, grow - ing wis - er. _____ And

Slower

we are grow - ing free. _____ We need you.

We are a fam - i - ly. _____

DREAMGIRLS

Music by HENRY KRIEGER
Lyric by TOM EYEN

Life's not as bad _____ as it may seem if you o- pen your eyes _____ to what's in

front of you. _____

DREAMS:
We're your dream - girls, _____ boys. _____

DEENA:

_____ We'll make you hap - py.

DREAMS:
We're your

dream - girls, _____ boys. _____

DEENA:
We'll al - ways care. _____

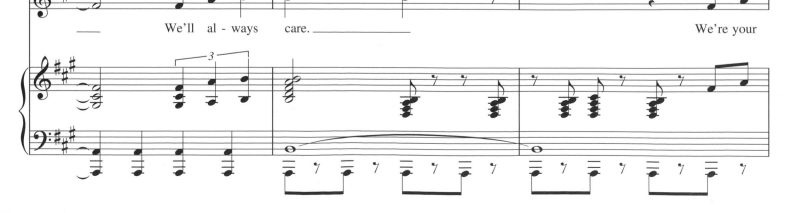

be-fore. _____ I'm the dream that will give _____ you more _____ and more. _____

DREAMS: We're your dream - girls, _ boys. _ We'll make you

hap - py. We're your dream - girls, _ boys. _

DEENA: We'll al - ways care. _____ **DREAMS:** We're your

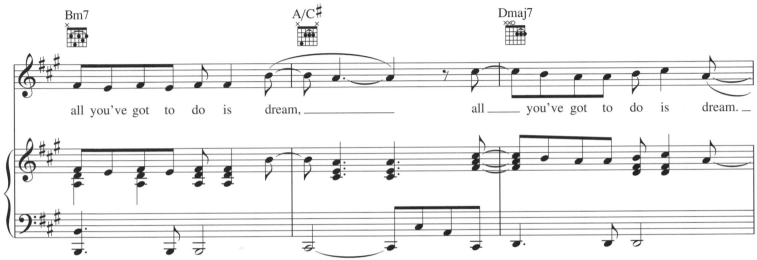

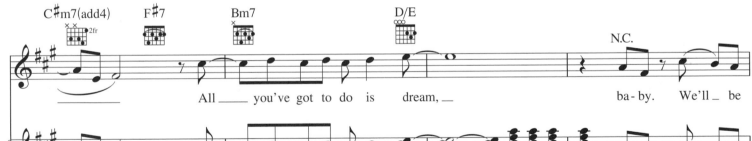

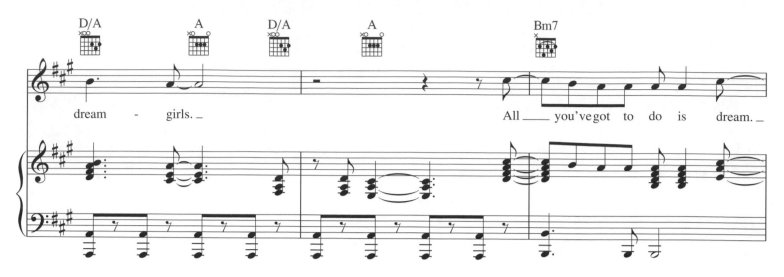

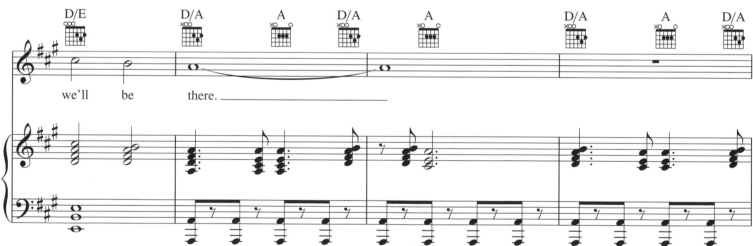

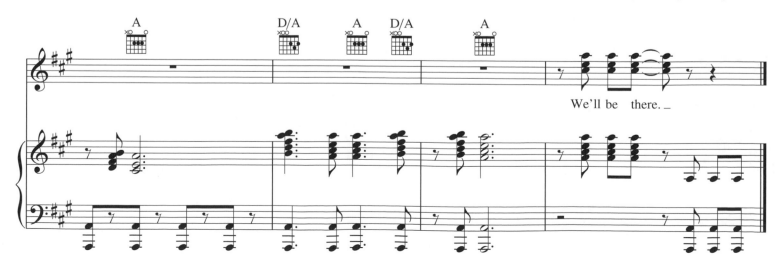

AND I AM TELLING YOU
I'M NOT GOING

Music by HENRY KRIEGER
Lyric by TOM EYEN

Moderately

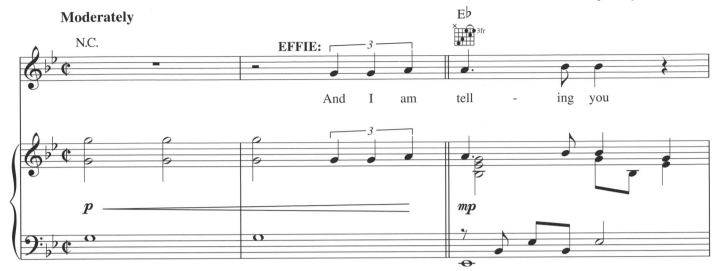

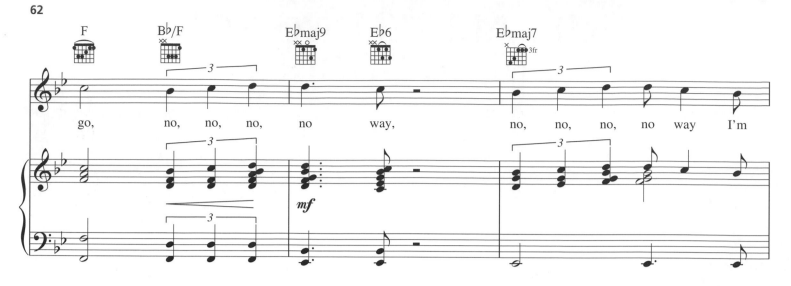

go, no, no, no, no way, no, no, no, no way I'm

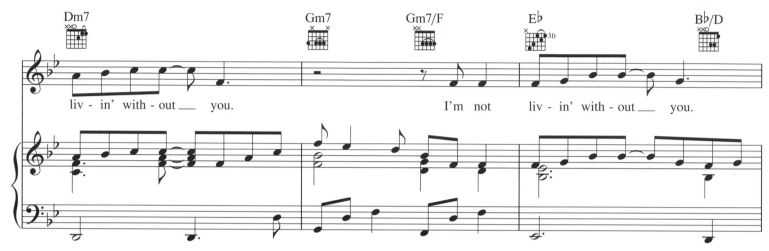

liv - in' with - out ___ you. I'm not liv - in' with - out ___ you.

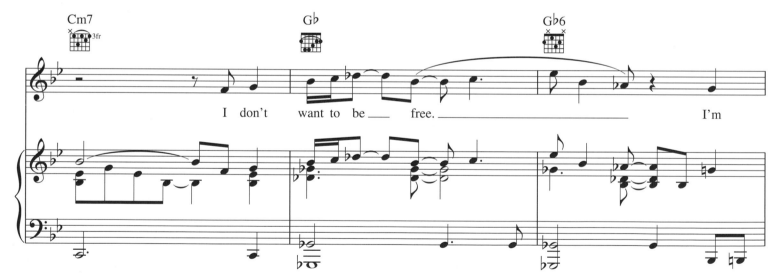

I don't want to be ___ free. ___ I'm

stay - in', ___ I'm stay - in', and you, and you,

you're gon - na love ___ me. _____ Ooh, ___

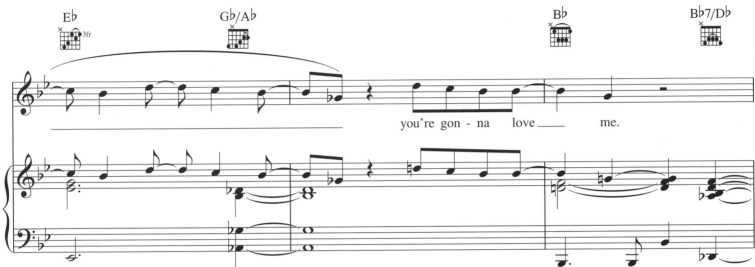

you're gon - na love ___ me.

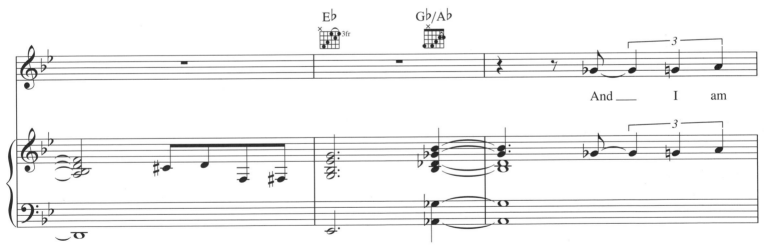

And ___ I am

tell - ing you I'm not go - ing, ___ Ooh,

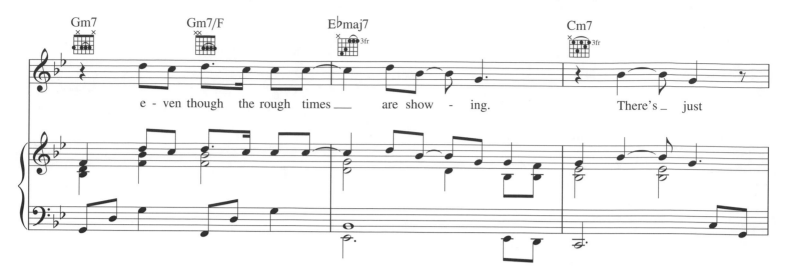

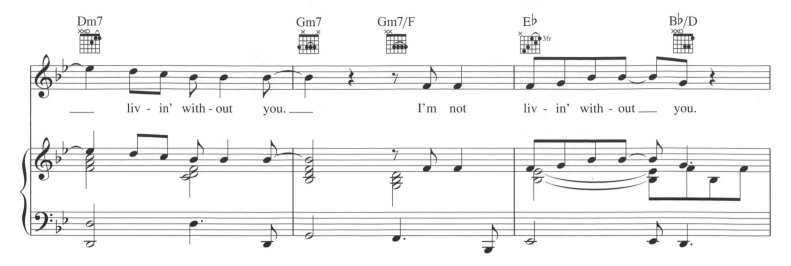

liv - in' with - out you. ___ I'm not liv - in' with - out ___ you.

You see, there's just no way, there's no ___ way. ___

Funky

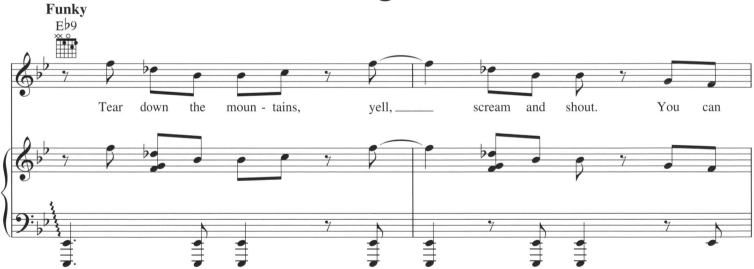

Tear down the moun - tains, yell, ___ scream and shout. You can

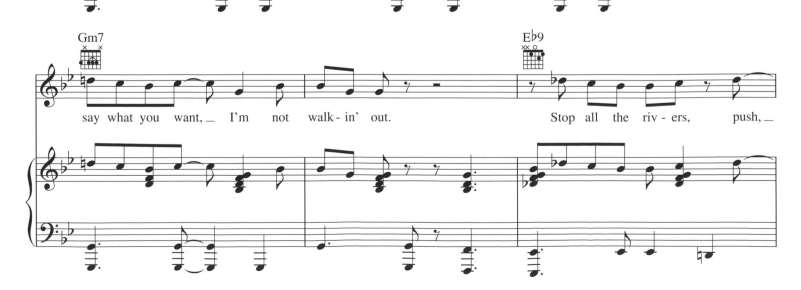

say what you want, __ I'm not walk - in' out. Stop all the riv - ers, push, __

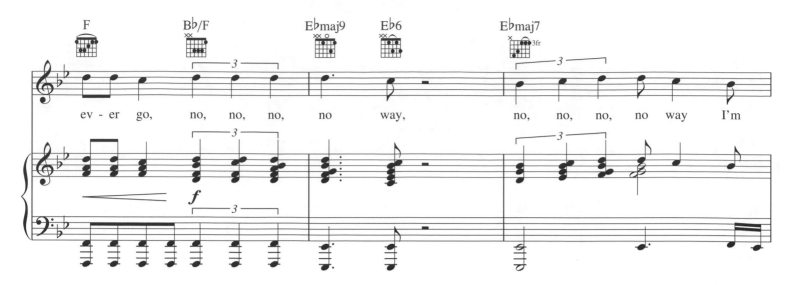

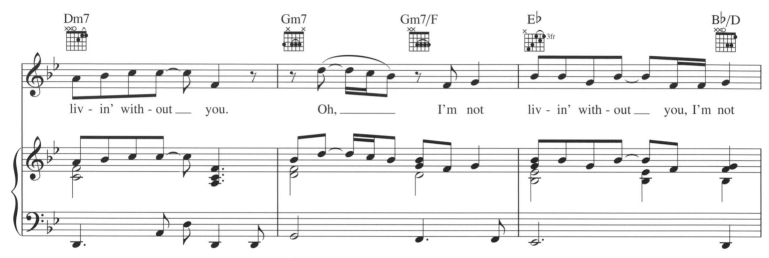

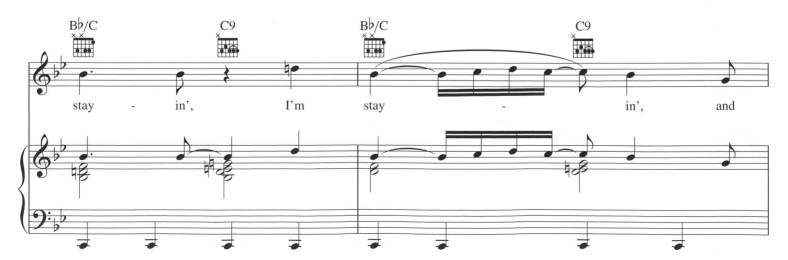

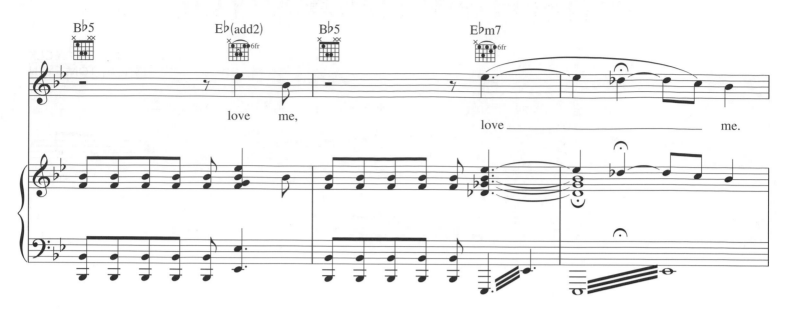

love me,   love _____ me.

Freely
N.C.

You're gon - na love _____

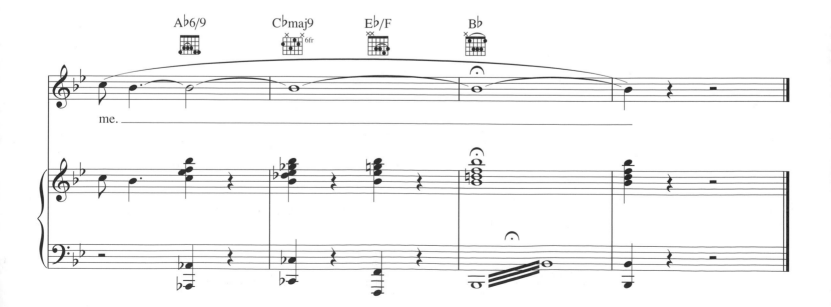

me. _____

WHEN I FIRST SAW YOU

Music by HENRY KRIEGER
Lyric by TOM EYEN

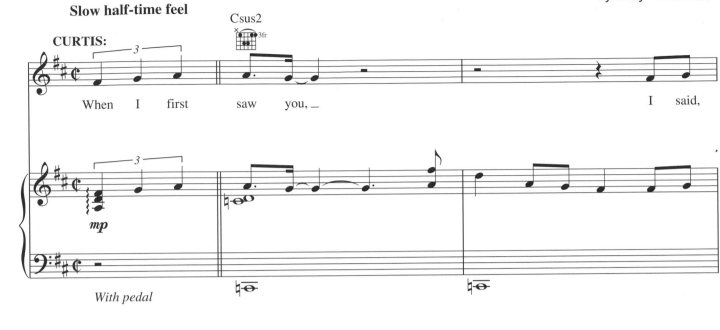

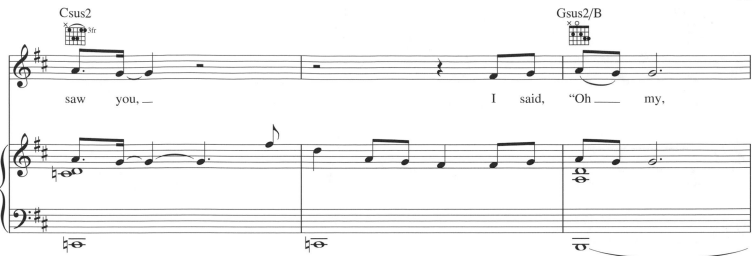

saw you, __ I said, "Oh __ my,

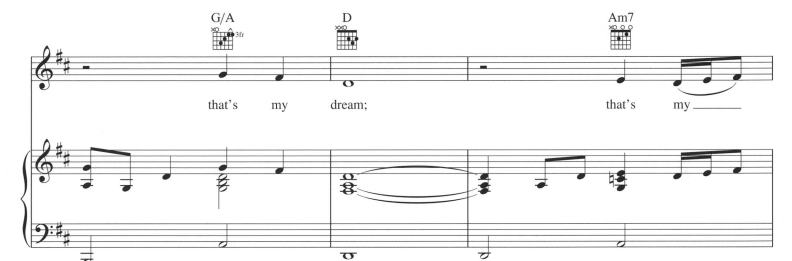

that's my dream; that's my __

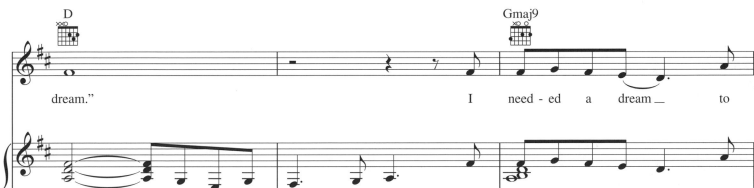

dream." I need-ed a dream __ to

make me strong. __ You were the on - ly

world ____ would be - lieve in my dreams __ too? _____ Be -

CURTIS:

fore you ap - peared, life was on - ly a game, __

and day in _____ and day out _____ were the

same. _____ Now the dream's com - ing

DEENA:

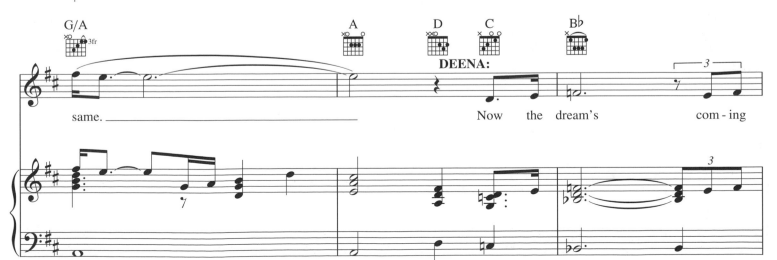

PATIENCE

Music by HENRY KRIEGER
Lyrics by WILLIE REALE

When will come the morn - ing to drive the night _ a - way? _ Tell me,

when will come the morn - ing of a bright - er day? _

Oh, _ pa - tience, _ lit - tle

sis - ter. _ Pa - tience, _ lit - tle

broth - er. ____ Pa - tience, __ pa - tience; ____

take each oth - er by the hand.

Oh, ____ pa - tience, __ lit - tle

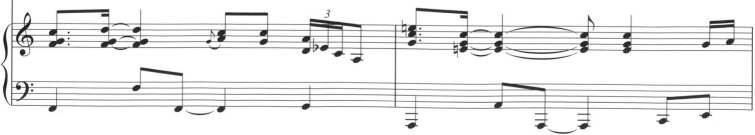

sis - ters, ____ pa - tience, __ lit - tle

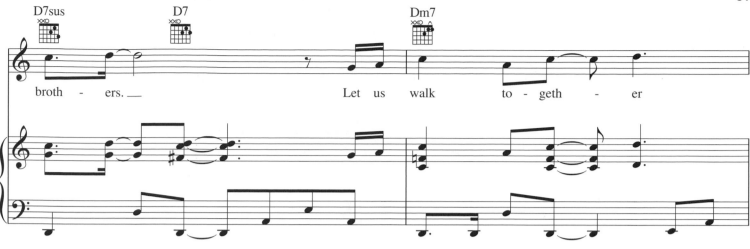

broth - ers. ___   Let us walk to - geth - er

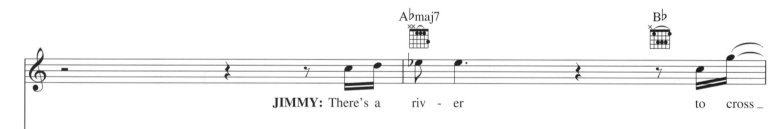

to the prom - ised land. ___

JIMMY: There's a riv - er   to cross ___

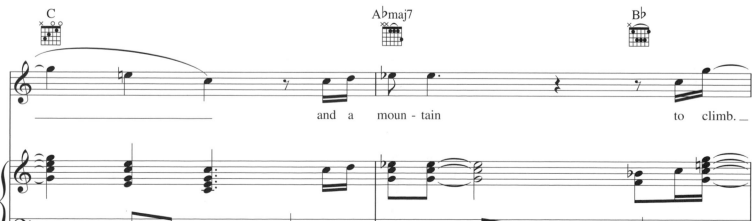

___   and a moun - tain   to climb. ___

Pa - tience,___ pa - tience;___

it's gon-na take some time.

LORRELL: We must walk in

peace._____ It's the on - ly, on -

broth - er. Pa - tience, _ pa - tience. _

BOTH: We're gon - na find a way. _

LORRELL: Pa - tience, _ **JIMMY:** lit - tle

sis - ters. Pa - tience, _ lit - tle

broth - ers, ___ un - til that morn, ___ yeah, yeah, ___

___ **BOTH:** of a bright - er day. ___

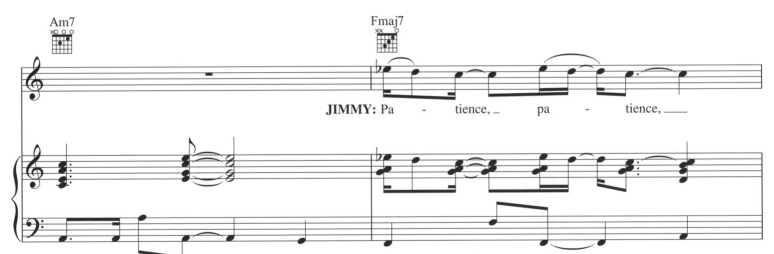

JIMMY: Pa - tience, _ pa - tience, ___

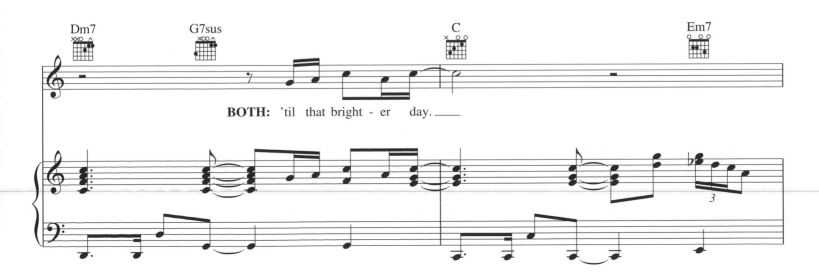

BOTH: 'til that bright - er day. ___

LORRELL: Oh, pa - tience

BOTH: 'til that bright - er day. ____

Lead vocals ad lib. to end

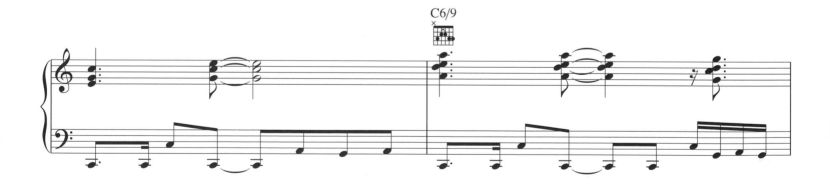

I AM CHANGING

Music by HENRY KRIEGER
Lyric by TOM EYEN

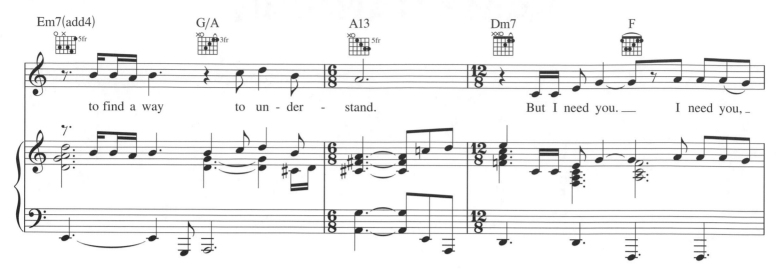

to find a way   to un - der - stand.   But I need you. __   I need you, __

I need __ a hand. _____   I _____ am chang - ing,

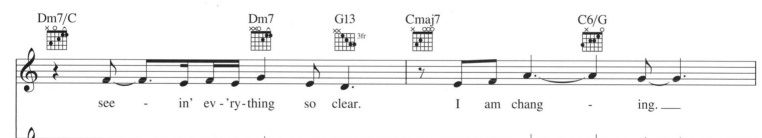

see - in' ev - 'ry-thing so clear.   I am chang - ing. __

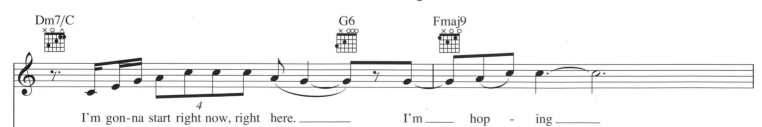

I'm gon-na start right now, right here. _____   I'm __ hop - ing _____

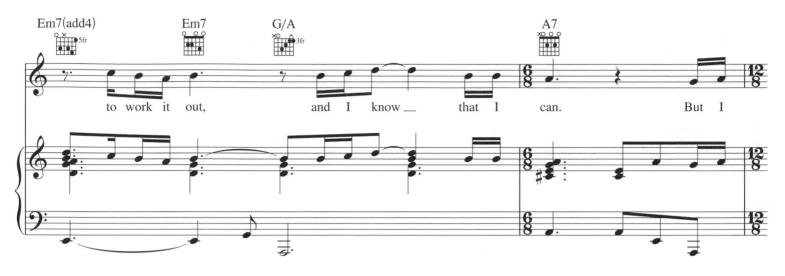

to work it out, and I know __ that I can. But I

need _____ you. I need a hand.

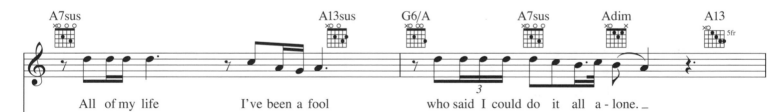

All of my life I've been a fool who said I could do it all a - lone. __

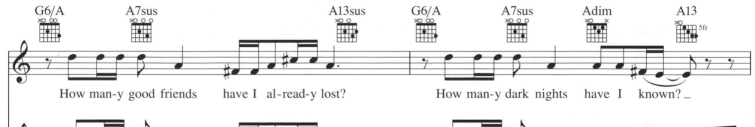

How man-y good friends have I al-read-y lost? How man-y dark nights have I known? __

PERFECT WORLD

Music by HENRY KRIEGER
Lyrics by SIEDAH GARRETT

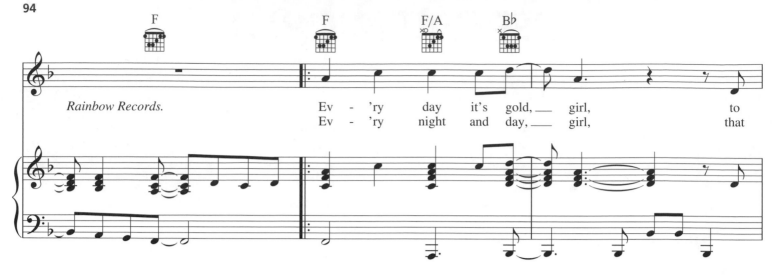

but } I know I'm in love ___ with you, ___ { but you don't
                                           and you don't

e - ven know ___ my name. ___ }
e - ven know ___ I'm a - live. ___ }   Girl meets boy, boy ___

___ meets girl. ___ They could fall ___ in love in a per - fect world, _ but if

boy and girl nev - er meet, ___ then a per - fect world can nev -

ONE NIGHT ONLY

Music by HENRY KRIEGER
Lyric by TOM EYEN

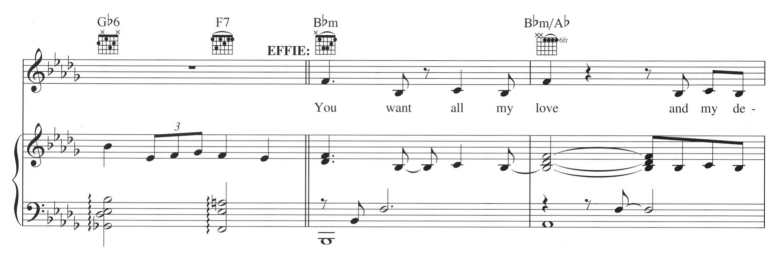

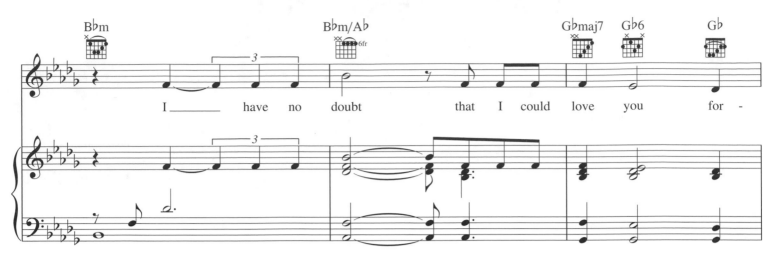

I _____ have no doubt that I could love you for-

ev - er. The on - ly trou - ble is _____ you

real - ly don't have the time. ____ You've got one night on - ly,
One night on - ly,

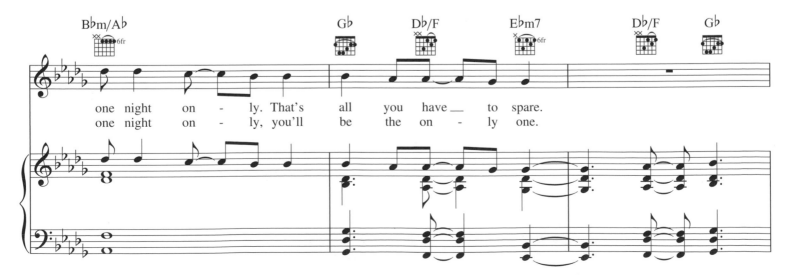

one night on - ly. That's all you have ___ to spare.
one night on - ly, you'll be the on - ly one.

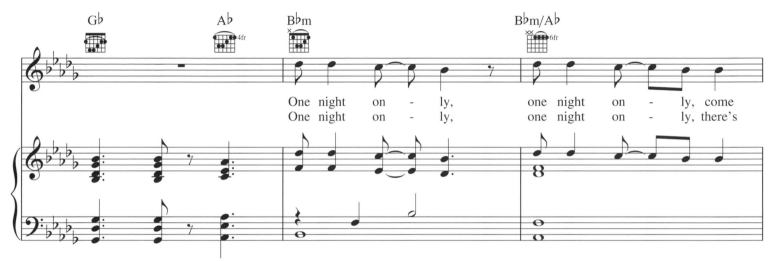

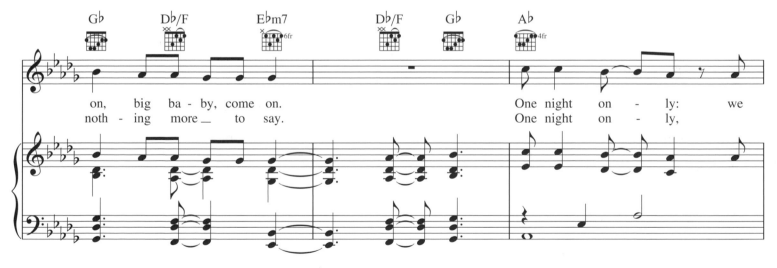

morn - ing, this feel - ing will be gone. It

has no chance go - ing on.

Some - thing so right has got no chance to live.

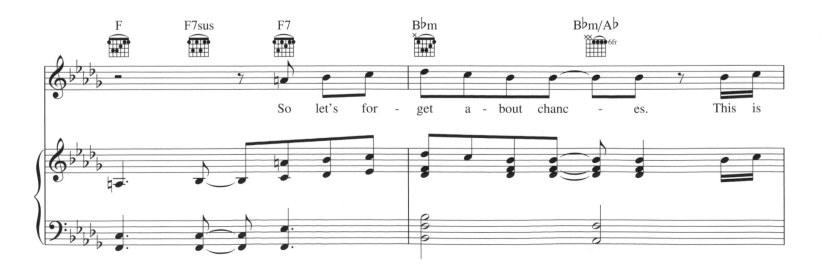

So let's for - get a - bout chanc - es. This is

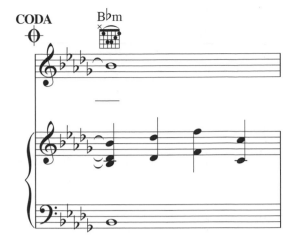

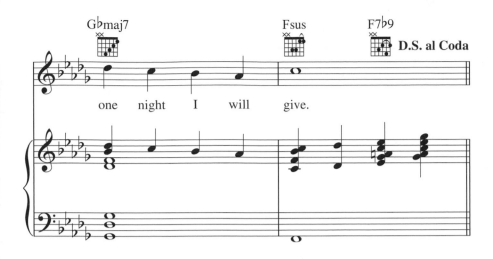

LISTEN

Music and Lyrics by HENRY KRIEGER, ANNE PREVEN,
SCOTT CUTLER and BEYONCE KNOWLES

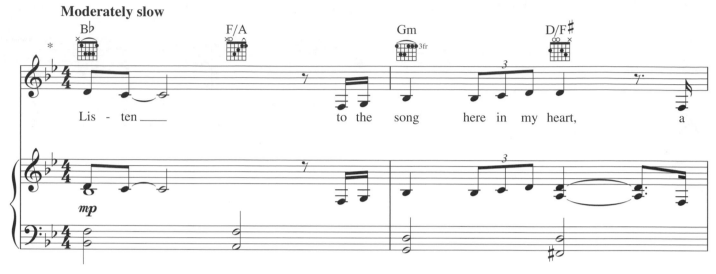

Moderately slow

Lis - ten ____ to the song here in my heart, a

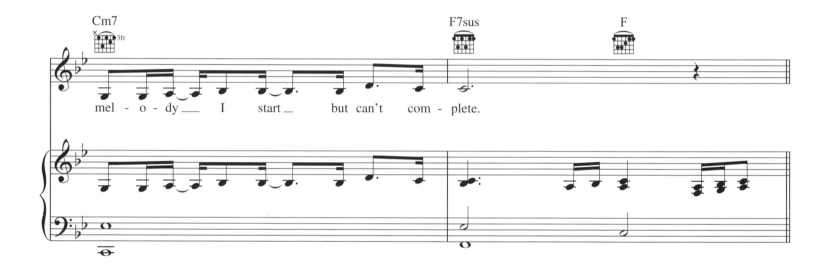

mel - o - dy ____ I start ____ but can't com - plete.

Lis - ten ____ to the sound from deep with - in. It's

lis - tened. ____ There is some - one here in - side, some -

* *Recorded a half step higher.*

but now I've got-ta find _____ my own. I don't ___ know where I be-long, ___ but

I'll be mov-ing on. _____ If you don't, if you

won't, _____ lis - ten _____ to the

song here in my heart, a mel - o - dy ___ I start, ___ but I _____

HARD TO SAY GOODBYE,
MY LOVE

Music by HENRY KRIEGER
Lyric by TOM EYEN

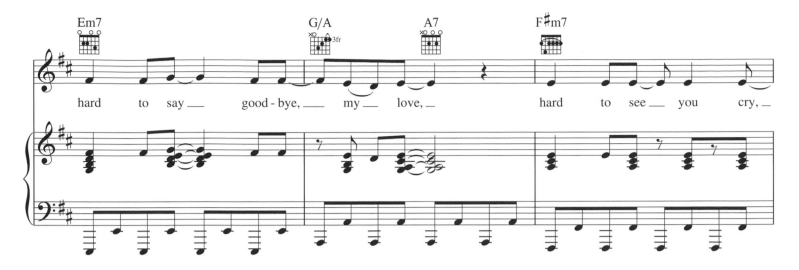

hard to say ___ good-bye, ___ my ___ love, ___ hard to see ___ you ___ cry, ___

___ my love; ___ hard to o - pen up that door ___ when

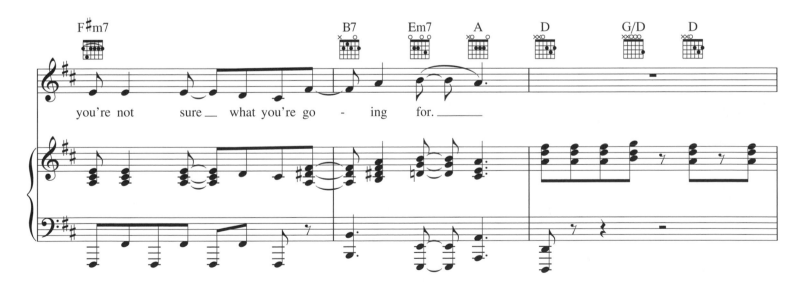

you're not sure ___ what you're go - ing for. _____

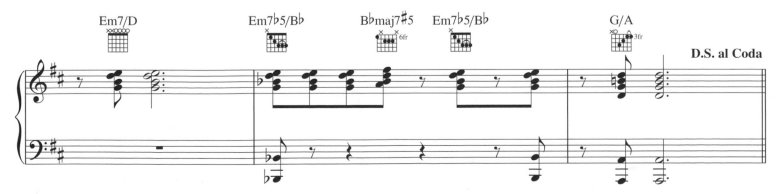

D.S. al Coda

110

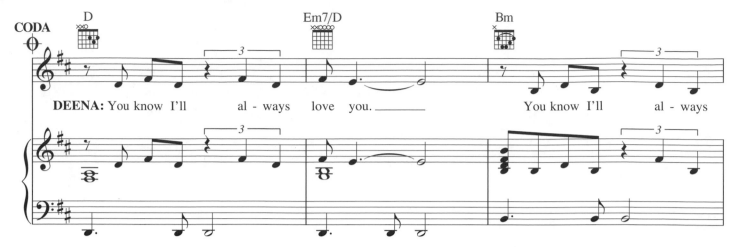

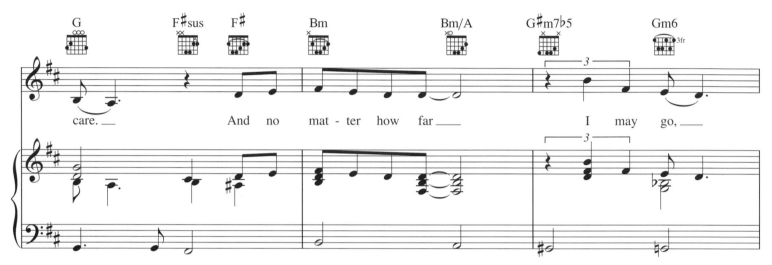

hard to see __ you cry, __ my love; __ hard to o - pen up

that door __ when you're not sure __ what you're go - ing for. __ But

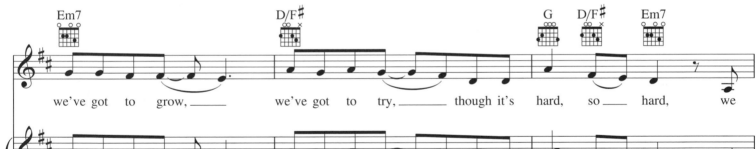

we've got to grow, __ we've got to try, __ though it's hard, so __ hard, we

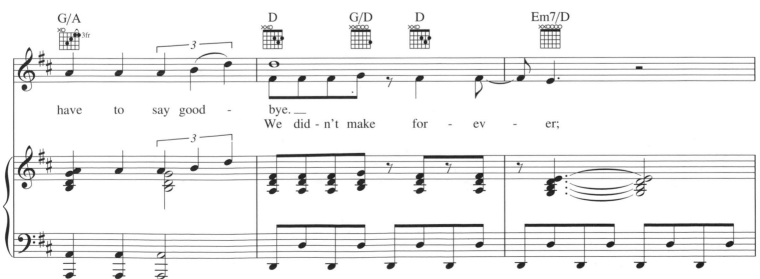

have to say good - bye. __
We did - n't make for - ev - er;

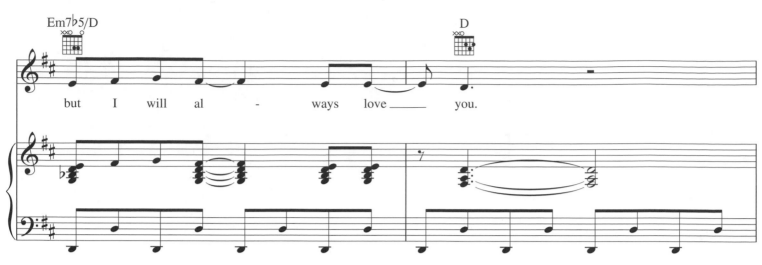

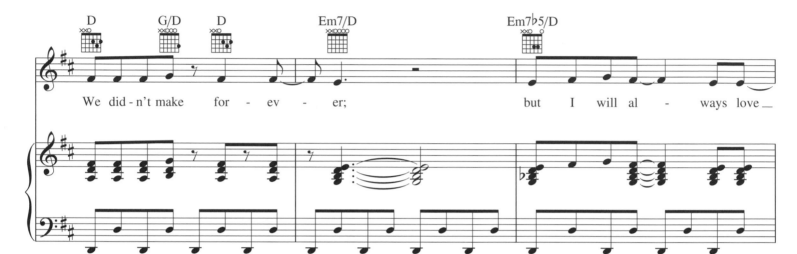

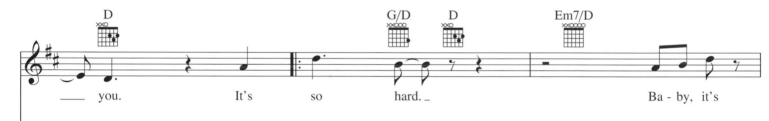

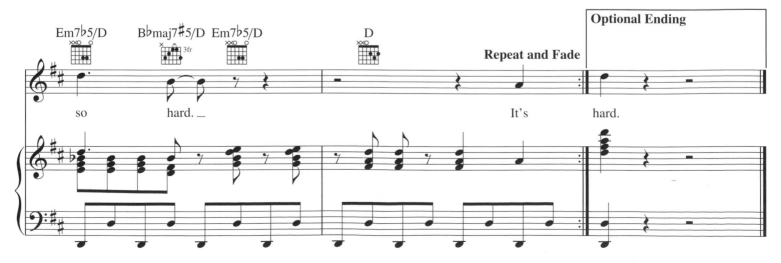